MW01240699

Acknowledgements

God, you are my everything without you I am nothing. So first, to you I want to say thank you Jesus Christ my Lord and savior. To my children Jason my oldest and most loyal son, you are my motivation to win. To my Daughter, My Tiffany you are my smile in the time of adversity thank you beautiful. To Jaylen, you are rock, thank you for being the most humbled and grateful child, I can't wait to give you the world. I love you. To Alphonzo and Alan you are mommy's joy, thank you for praying for me and showing me unconditional love.

To my biological adopted daughter Nikki, I thank God for your pure heart to forgive me. I'm very proud of you, love you (Ha). To my other daughter Lisa until we meet again, you are never forgotten, I love you. To my grandson's Chase and Justyn this one is for you and to my darling granddaughter Logan I love you.

To my God daughter Shola Oni, you are heaven sent. Thank you for helping me birth this book and believing in me.

To my Mother thank you for your love and support. To my dad (rih) you taught me how to be kind and to laugh uncontrollably, I miss you. To my grandmother you are my angel, you are everything a grandmother should be and much more. Thank you for teaching me about Jesus and sharing your name with me, (Pat) I love you.

To Dr. Pastor Vincent Matthews, you taught me what a man of integrity looks like thank you.

To Bishop DeRose and Apostle Greg Davis you men have set a standard and made a mark on my life, My humbled thanks.

To Evangelist Valerie Parks, you're my sister for real thank you. To Kiesha Downer thank you for teaching me about faith through your testimonies. To my prayer line family, leaders who supported me and prayed for me, love you all and thank you.

Table of Contents

Table of Contents Continue:

Some of the character names has been changed to protect the identify of those mentioned. The format in the testimonies are written but not in any chronological order of events, it's in the order lead by his Holy Spirit. All testimonies are true and not revised.

Nora Jones Ministries

THE NORA JONES STORY

TRUE TESTIMONIES OF TRANSFORMATION

So never be ashamed to tell others about our Lord. And don't be ashamed of me, either, even though I'm in prison for him. With the strength God gives you, be ready to suffer with me for the sake of the Good news. For God saved us and called us to live a holy life. He did this, not because we deserved it, but because that was his plan from before the beginning of time-to show us his grace through Jesus Christ.

- 2 Timothy 1:8-9 NLT

One

One day I was watching a YouTube video of a lady testifying about her life and how she went through a hard life and God turned it around. I remember as if it was yesterday. I cried and instantly felt attached to this lady, because I identified with her TESTIMONY, I identified with her pain. Instantly the holy spirit begins to speak to me, "Nora I want you to make a video". I dismissed the instruction, but was so intrigue with this brave solider who would display to the world her shortcomings…. who was this woman I thought? I instantly became a Facebook stalker, confession is good for the soul, right? LOL, Well I went on to her page and begin to look at her pictures. I remember even putting up her photo next to mine and posted it as if we were sisters, because we had similar hair styles
and posed the same on the photo. It was as if the TESTIMONY bonded us like glue.

So, a few days later, I went on to her page just to see her updated stats and I noticed it was another YouTube video on her page but this time it wasn't her. The comments said it was her friend from school but the video was like hers, no talking, just writing on a poster board that read of the pain, triumphs and victory. There was gospel music playing in the background, it was just an awesome video of God's hand on her life.

Again, the holy spirit spoke "She did it, you can too". I decided this time I must obey, within an hour we had boards that read "I sold my body for money", "I've been depressed all my life", "My boys were molested by my gay family member".

My son recorded the video, he was 13 at the time. Shockingly, he didn't judge me or question me which help me to complete the 3 minute YouTube video. My emotions were heavy and I cried during the entire video as I posted almost every card. It was like a bunch of painful memories had resurfaced but the joy of the Lord was my strength, finally I was done.

I went to church that night, it was bible study and afterward I was ready to show my pastor and first lady, besides God told me to do it. I'm wasn't ashamed and I knew I must be obedient. As they watched some of the words were hard to read because of my penmanship so I read it off to them, they said Nora we are proud of you. Wow, we didn't know that but we are proud of you coming forth. I was glad that they didn't judge me and seemed to understand why I must post this video.

After bible study, I got in my truck and cried. I called my boyfriend at the time who was also on the poster card, it read "I have a boyfriend who accepts me for who I am". I called Dave, while in tears and as always, he tried to console me as best he could over the phone. What's wrong he asked? Well, I showed the video to my pastor and first lady they support me but wanted me to rewrite it so it can be legible but it's something wrong, I don't feel right. I didn't tell it all in that video!

Ok, he said that's ok. NO!! I exclaimed, if your following God you must keep it real and tell it all. Ok, Nora so just tell it all he suggested. I CAN'T DO THAT!! I said admittedly!! Why not Dave said? Just tell it all. Well it's somethings nobody knows, it's secrets from my past. Well let me tell you and if I can tell you then I can tell the anybody.

Well, everyone knows I put my baby up for adoption but nobody knows it was two babies (tears flowing). I had a baby and got pregnant again right afterwards giving both up for adoption, I kept it a secret. All I heard was extreme laughter. Wait, why are you laughing? Man, I thought you was going to say you was an alien or something. (blank stare) what? I laughed through the tears.

That dumb joke cleaned my soul, I knew if he didn't judge me the world couldn't either. I went back in the house that night and I told it ALL!! I made a new video and added these poster cards "I have seven kids, with seven daddies," "I have a baby by an 89-year-old trick". The music played Take Me to The King.

Thus, The Nora Jones Story was birthed, that was almost 4 years ago. My story didn't end there it has just begin...

I will declare your righteousness and your salvation every day, though I do not fully understand what the outcome will be. Lord God, I will come in the power of your mighty acts, remembering your righteousness—yours alone.

Psalms 71:15-16

Two

Within two weeks of airing the Nora Jones Story on YouTube, I received three miracles. Yes, you heard me right I said three miracles that I am convinced I only received them with my obedience to TELL IT ALL, in my video.

First Miracle... I got an inbox on Facebook, and it read something like this. I'm your daughter you put up for adoption 18 years ago, I don't know if you want to speak with me but I thought I would reach out. I remember reading it as if I heard her attitude come out in the words, she was my daughter. I couldn't wait to reply, yes, I want to talk to you call me. She replied call you now? I said YES!! That was the longest 2 minutes of my life.

I believe it was around 8pm or so and I remember talking to her at least 4 hours straight. It was my baby Nikki, the one I choose parents for so everyone knew about her.

I was anxious to hear about her life and praying she wouldn't hate me. She spoke proper and was very intelligent, she was more then what I prayed for over the years. I couldn't wait to reconnect.

Later that morning, it was my first speaking engagement since the video. I was scheduled to speak while the church was showing my testimony video on a projector screen, so this was a huge moment for me. The blessing of speaking within a church congregation as we watch the testimony video together.

I told my daughter Nikki about the engagement and that I would love for her to join me. She agreed and with little almost no sleep I drove the almost 2-hour drive one way to pick her up.

The meeting was emotional and joyful, this young lady was graduating soon and she was so beautiful. I was so proud. We talked the entire drive back to my house to get ready for service. She enjoyed meeting her other siblings, 4 brothers and 1 sister all of which I raised. Her sister Tiffany was only a few years older. They seemed to bond instantly. The girls and I headed to church and you can only imagine my adrenaline level. No sleep, meeting my daughter and speaking, while sharing my testimony. To God be the glory, I was ecstatic in my spirit!!

The service was amazing, it was an extra blessing that the pastor and first lady was my cousins, other family was there as well. Everyone came to support me and to see my daughter for the first time. It was even more special when I shared my testimony of my daughter been present after our meeting for the first time that day, it was a surreal moment in my life, that God allowed me to be blessed with.

You can call it luck for our reconnection but for it to happen only days after my video post, I knew it was a miracle. I could attend her graduation too, God is an on-time God.

Three

Second Miracle... I decided to leave my 5-year-old son with my grandmother as my fiancé and I along with my older children went to cedar point with my CWA coworkers from my job. Upon returning the next day, I picked up my son as we preceded to get ready to go to the CWA union picnic which was that day. I pulled into the mall parking lot ready to go shopping and I noticed something was wrong with my son. He seemed quiet and sad. So, I asked him what's wrong? He begins to tell me about his uncle touching his private, and he cried uncontrollably.

My uncle was openly gay but I would have never thought he would do this despicable act. I confronted him because kids don't lie. Not at that age and he had details. My uncle of course denied it but I did what any mother would do, I believed my child. Let me say this, my uncle and I was like best friends.

He was openly gay but we all accepted him although he apparently liked younger boys. For some reason, nobody would say anything if he bought a 17-year-old to our family BBQ and he was 45 years old Introducing him his friend. I can't explain it, I was also guilty of looking the other way on such odd situations.

He was my favorite uncle, funny and gossipy and everyone loved his outgoing demeanor. So, when this molestation allegation came out, I was hurt beyond words. I still am, I don't know if you every repair from such a thing, you just find a way to cope and heal, but the void of betrayal of trust and the why?? remains.

After an investigation, I was told because there wasn't any penetration and my son was so young he couldn't be a reliable witness because of his age. I was devastated!! My family seemed to still take their kids around him after severe warnings from me. They seemed to want to push it under the rug, besides this was a taboo subject and this was the fun uncle everybody liked, so it's better if we don't talk about it, they felt.

Shortly afterwards I learned that my other son was molested to by the same uncle, again he denied. I begin to do things like drive over there and try to fight him, only to be kicked out by my grandmother and to be chased out her house with a broom and being called crazy. I was crazy, I had lost my mind in hurt, I was lost.

The counselor suggested we stay away from my grandmother's house because that was the house the incident happened in and he still lived there. What? you want me to not go to grandma's? Everybody goes to grandma's, that's where the tasty food is, the BBQ's and family fun happens there. That's all we knew is grandma's house. I was discombobulated with pain, confusion and ANGER!!!

I'm going to kill him, I told my mom. I planned it out, I was prepared to go to jail and I told her I'm killing him tomorrow at 6am. I believe around 5am the next day, I opened the door and the first thing my mother said is don't kill

him. I remember thanking God because I knew he sent her, she knew I was serious but God had something better for me then jail.
The Spirit of the Lord told me, if you don't kill him and give this to me you will see justice.

After been separated from my grandmother about 10 years, I got a call from my mother saying my uncle allegedly molested 2 brothers and they told their teacher and he was in jail. An hour later my brother called me crying and saying I'm going to kill him, I'm going to kill him. Finally, they BELIEVE ME!! After 10 long years, they finally believe me. For me, that was my miracle, that my family began calling and they believed me.

My uncle was released of that case because of lack of evidence. Then within a year later a case was filed charging him with fondling two other minor brothers. He was sentenced to three years in prison under a plea deal. Then it was almost 10 years of me not seeing my grandmother. Although we live in separate states now, we are inseparable. I have never questioned her loyalty to him, or told her of my pain. I just rather love her for the angel she is in my life and forgive her.

I remember being on my prayer line and we had a topic on forgiveness and I ministered the word and the callers and I cried together. I never knew so many people were dealing with un forgiveness. It was so profound, the following week we decided to do a part two. So, the day before our part 2 prayer line call. I was at church praying that God blesses the people who will call in tomorrow and that they forgive, use me Lord I remember asking. The spirit of the Lord said you haven't forgave. I remember getting defensive and questioning, who me? Lord I have forgiven. He said no you haven't, when you see your uncle picture on Facebook or on somebody's timeline you are always blocking them. You haven't forgiven your uncle.

I thought about it and begin to search my inner heart because if I'm a prophetess called to ministry and I can't do something I'm asking others to do, I wouldn't be a woman of integrity.

That night on the prayer line I forgave my uncle and made peace in my spirit because I understand God plan is bigger than ours and our ways is not his ways. He allowed me to experience this testimony so I can minister to other people who were affected by molestation.

About a year ago, I finally connected with the mother who kids were brave enough to testify against my uncle. Her story was way more tragic then mine, she lost custody of her boys because of this incident and now struggles with severe depression.

Sometimes, I don't know what to say when I speak with her and hearing her speak of the same pain I endured. I try to always remind her of her fight and how she can use to tragic situation as a testimony to her strength or as a memory to her demise.

She often says my uncle killed her and I often tell her no he doesn't have enough power to kill you, live through it. One day at a time, one prayer at a time.

We are forever connected by our
TESTIMONY, I will never forget her.

And when ye stand praying, forgive, if ye have ought against
any: that your Father also which is in heaven may forgive you
trespasses.

Mark 11:25

Four

Third Miracle... I started working for a multi-level marketing company called 5linx. I was scheduled to go to an opportunity meeting at a nearby hotel. I remember turning the corner and seeing what appeared to be hundreds of people to the left and right side of me, standing in long lines and a registration desk that seated 3 people. I walked up to the registration desk and before I could say my name, Calvin who invited me to this meeting says come on, I signed you in already.

The next few moments appeared to be a movie in slow motion, I begin to follow him and everyone stared. I could hear the whispers of people saying who is she, I kept walking in a slow motion as Calvin motioned me to come on, it seemed like this walk lasted forever.

People were looking at me like millionaire, I truly felt what it was like to be a millionaire, God allowed it. I know this sounds weird but I only can explain this as best I could, that walk wasn't just a walk it was God showing me my future and how it felt to be set apart.

Upon entering the conference room, I saw a large projector screen, chairs and 3 people who motioned me to come. I was the first guest in the room. I could sit anywhere I wanted I believe I was chosen by God to be a millionaire, I use to always say it but now I felt it. I thought maybe this opportunity was the reason God allowed me my prophetic moment so I joined the business. Within 3 weeks I had one of the fastest growing teams in Michigan with over 30 partners.

Success became my life and I soon disconnected my time with God, chasing money. My Sunday worship was replaced with opportunity meetings and personal business receptions. I would eat and drink 5linx and no one could tell me nothing. I told my pastor the day I signed up to 5linx, I will be a millionaire tither. I knew it, I felt it in my spirit now God has shown me in that prophetic vision so I was convinced 5linx was the way.

One day I was marketing my business on Facebook and a man in boxed me and wanted to know about the business opportunity. He was a truck driver and wanted to retire and gain wealth. He had a few kids and a baby on the way with his ex, but he wanted to make a fresh start not just with 5linx he was interested in me.

He said he saw my testimony video on YouTube and was proud of me, we chatted on the phone and he instantly became one of my business partners. I was at a cross road in my life, love had failed me. Dave, was seeing someone else and I was ready for a companion not necessarily love, I was just lonely. I mean besides the fact I got married at 22 and that love of my life was in jail most of those years and when he came home, he decided he couldn't forgive me for having kids outside of wedlock.

At the time, I wasn't sure if he loved me or just had love for me. I married him in jail but I've known him for a long time. He was my first love and boyfriend at 12 years old. In fact, we were the same age and shared the same birthdate. My love was true for him but I always felt like I couldn't measure up. I didn't feel good enough and he never helped my insecurity, he only made it worst.

He told me what to wear and how to wear my hair. He didn't know but just his gestures and words of why you wear that up here made me feel self-conscience. It was also hard not knowing when he would come home. At that time, he was given a 30-year sentence, so after 5 years mentally I couldn't deal with the expensive phone bills, and the lonely nights. So, we ended that relationship and later the marriage.

Now Years later here I was about to make one of the biggest mistakes of my life.

Tim filled my temporary void, I only needed companionship not love and after only 2 weeks of talking we decided to see each other. He was only 5'5 and I was 5'7 this was always my pet peeve dating shorter guys but at this point in my life my standard changed.

I only required for him to have a job and be Christian and he was both, so he said. After staying the night in a hotel, we decided confirmed we was going to get married. I was in my late 30's and he was in his early 30's and nobody had time to waste.

I wasn't so skeptical to marry without knowing him, I felt if we keep God first we could make it. But, I was skeptical about him having this baby on the way, so to reassure me he called his child's mother. She spoke so nice, as she explained he's a great guy, and a great dad and they won't be together besides raising the baby.

He loves you Nora, she proclaimed! He speaks wonderful things about you. Where do they do that at? The ex says wonderful things about a man, never had this happened before. That sealed the deal in my flesh and the only thing left was for me to do was pray and ask God, NOT!! I knew God wouldn't allow such a thing, I knew his holy spirit was going to convict me so I just asked God just to let me do this, and I know you will be there for me. I did the most selfish thing ever, decided I didn't need God permission.

One day Tim called and said baby, my truck is broken down here in Vegas, this is a sign from God let's do it now, let's get married. That day he wired me $500.00 by the next day I flew to Vegas, that weekend we were married.

I went on the road with him and after a week we settled back at my house only to get a message through Facebook that my new husband was still legally married, to his first wife. Yes, you heard me this guy was married! I was shocked and disappointed and of course very angry.

I comforted him and he left to go for a walk and never came back. He wasn't from Michigan, he was from Alabama so after 3 days I was concerned and I called his parents.

His dad told me, that Tim has issues of not liking conformation and he runs from everything. He was still legally married to his wife although they are not together but he has commitment issues. I was surprised of this revelation considering I spoke to his mom the night before we got married and she gave us well wishes.

Never the less this guy was miles away from home, his 18-wheeler truck was in the shop nearby me and he was missing and no one was worried except me.

Later I saw on fb he was with the baby's mom, the post said one big happy family. We were still within a month of getting married, we were newlyweds. I was furious and hurt. I messaged her to ask her why would you tell me, he loves me and you're with him. Why send us well wishes on getting married, if you still wanted him? She said, look let me tell you the truth, you were a part of a plot to get your money. We know you had money or you would be getting it soon from 5linx so Tim told me to say that and he played you.

I went into a downward depression, with him still calling me saying he is coming home and he was divorcing her, playing mind games. Finally, I stop taking his calls but nothing could get me out of my homicidal, suicidal thoughts. I wanted to kill him then myself. Life was over for me. I was embarrassed, my 5linx peers was shocked I married this guy who wasn't even physically my type.

My family thought I was nuts, my children was tired of my men choices and vowed to not bond with another man. I was hurt, I told God I'm jumping over the balcony and the spirit of the Lord said no go on Facebook. The holy spirit had me looking for my child hood friend. This was stupid, I thought. I've been looking for him for years. But, within 3 mins I found him, God allowed me to find him and he ministered to my spirit by letting me have it. I mean he said what's wrong with you? You still doing dumb stuff? Your dad would have never agreed to that. He said, "it's been 20 years and you're still doing the same thing". This wasn't just anyone who was talking, this was the man that my daddy loved and admired. My dad had died 10 years ago by this time, so Carl meant a lot to us.

This was the same man my daddy told to marry me someday because he knew, he loved me. Even at 16 years old my dad saw something in this man when he was 18 years old that I rarely see in men today and that was pure love of Jesus Christ. Although it wasn't a reunion of reconnection of love, it was God who sent a man who really loved me. He loved me enough to tell me the truth, and it saved my life. God gave me just what I needed, when I needed it and from whom I can accept it from. JESUS SAVED ME!!

The Miracle in this was not only did God save me, he revealed my future.

Why did Tim come in my life to marry me for money that I don't have? Because, Satan peeked into my future and saw it. I never use to ask God to be a millionaire, I asked God to be a millionaire tither.

My Miracle was God SAVED me from suicide and showed me what's to come. Ever since my null in void marriage to Tim, I have never ever dated or had a relationship without asking God. I have learned to not move without Jesus.

I have also learned to not chase money, I chase God now and he sends the money. I understand the voids that I experienced through lack of a close relationship with my mother, and my father living out of state affected me socially. It effected my relationships with men because I was always searching for love because my mother never hugged and kissed us, she was more of a provider, and worked a lot. So, I would always be extra loving to a man, although I didn't require it back.

Most often our issues we have in relationships steams from the lack we had as children situations or tragedy's we experienced growing up. I kept repeating the same cycle year after year because I thought it was the men but it was ME.

How we view a thing is how it's viewed. We must get into a position and let God show us the angle, he gives us the best view.

Before you date or enter a business commitment make sure you're in a good posture to hear from God, otherwise you will have more and more TESTIMONIES but no TRANSFORMATIONS.

Jesus answered, "Even if I do bear witness about myself, my testimony is true, for I know where I came from and where I am going, but you do not I know where I come from or where I am going.

John 8: 14

Five

I remember all my life, I always felt displaced. I always felt weird and different. I remember walking in the mall and feeling like everybody was staring, I was young teenager and I couldn't shake that feeling of feeling out of place.

It wasn't until my early 20's when my grandmother introduced me to church and I was baptized, I begin to come to know Jesus. During that time, I knew him as my God but not my Lord. What I mean is God was blessing me but I wouldn't surrender my all to him, this means he wasn't my Lord but I was his daughter.

I was robbed by gunpoint and raped by gun point and raped again and beat, but I didn't die. I was humiliated, sad, depressed, angry, felt broken but I didn't die. Not only did I not die, I witnessed blessings after blessings after blessings.

I never suffered a day in the hospital after being raped and tortured, I never had broken bones during any physical altercation and I was always in my right mind. I mean that situation never allowed me to lose my mind, no matter what situation occurred tragically in my life God's hand was always on my life.

When I was 36, I was pregnant and found myself homeless. I went into a shelter because I wasn't comfortable laying on anybody couch after having children molested. I was cautious and the shelter made me feel as though that was my best move as a parent. When I got there, I got reconnected with someone I knew in elementary school, her name was Kim. She was cool and we connected instantly.

I was depressed and pregnant and I lost everything at my old house, when they put all my stuff outside. We had no clothes, no money and very little faith. I had unemployment as my only source of income, so I felt discouraged that I wouldn't be able to save to move into a new home.

Kim, was always smiling and laughing and one day I asked her, why you so happy we in a shelter. She reminded me that we are living in a place we have no rent, we can shop and save money and she begin to laugh and say God is good. You couldn't help but laugh at the situation once being around Kim. Her perspective in life was very positive and it came at just the time I needed it.

I asked Kim about church and how was everybody getting there, she mentioned a lady comes into the shelter and pray with us, you should go to her church. I knew I needed God I was stressed and without much hope. I called the number that they gave me for the church van. That Sunday we stood outside of the shelter waiting for the van to pull up, it was three people from the shelter going but when the van pulled up it was a different name on van then the church I was referred to, so I told one of the girls I wasn't going. I wanted to go to the church that the lady comes out to minister. I don't want to go to a different church I said. The girl encouraged me, just go Nora she said. It says they are Baptist on the van, ok I said and we went to church. I instantly felt like I was at home at this church but I decided I would join after attending three Sundays. I had the same pink skirt on every Sunday but everyone hugged me, loved on the kids and showed me tremendous love.

I soon learned that was the church where a lady would come in and minister, so I joined. I joined her Sunday school class and instantly connected with her and joined ministries. I was going to church and feeling better but I still didn't have a plan to get a house other than section 8 which the entire shelter applied.

One day I was having a Debbie downer moment, that's a moment in which we are negative. So here comes Kim smiling and laughing I told her I was discouraged my income was not enough to move into a house, it was 6 weeks I've been in the shelter and I was ready to go. She laughed and told me, you don't need money to get a house you just need faith.

Kim begin to share her testimony of how God blessed her with a house with no money. I said you were just lucky and I went into my room. Kim would often testify to the goodness of Jesus Christ but a house with no money, that was just luck I thought. But, I had enough faith to start being positive. I started to volunteer for Saint Vincent DePaul call center which allowed me to get clothes and a bus pass to get out the shelter during the day.

I would catch the bus in the cold to go volunteer and I felt great. My life was looking up and I felt good about myself.

One night I called my ex, although he wasn't the father of my baby I was expecting he was the father of my other son and when I got pregnant he begged me to not have an abortion and vowed to help me. I called him to ask him for just a few dollars for bus fare, all I heard was laughter from a woman.

When I asked, who is this, she begin to tease me. HA you're in a shelter, your stupid Ha, Ha. I hung up the phone feeling humiliated, and

I cried out to God to please let me get over him and not love him anymore. Please help me GOD I CRIED!! DeCarlo's, has always been I huge strong hold for me. Although we had broken up years ago, I stilled loved him although he was mentally abusive. So, in this prayer I cried for God to release my heart from him.

My time in the shelter begin to be a positive one, I spoke of Jesus a lot and just like Kim I begin to be positive and encouraging. There was a girl there and her baby was disabled and I really felt sorry for her, but I knew she didn't like me. I wasn't mad about it. All my life some people primarily females didn't like me and I never understood that because I have a loving spirit.

One morning I was in the office of the shelter trying to fax a document and that girl was there, let's call her pam because for the life of me I can't remember her name. Well Pam was in the office to and it was a secretary lady sitting at the table. So, Pam begin to talk, I assumed she was talking to the lady at the desk. She said I hate it here, and begin to sop uncontrollably and although I knew she didn't like me I was the type of person I love people, so I had total compassion. I turned around and said," it will be ok Jesus loves you and he doesn't give you too much to handle". Pam instantly turned around and said mom, that's what I'm talking about this b@&$# all in my business.

She was on the phone I noticed, I said sorry I was just trying to help. She continued to call me names as I told her I wasn't going to be to many B#%^*@. Well she charged at me, and although people caught us before it became physical I was called into the office.

Nora, didn't we tell you to stop talking to people about Jesus, you can't do that here! Didn't we tell you to mind your business? I was just trying to help, I exclaimed. Nora, you must leave you can't stay here anymore.

I went to my room to cry and pack, I had nowhere to go and I was in shock. Before I could finish packing, outside my door was so many ladies who were all in tears. Nora, they kicking you out they asked? Yes, but I will be ok. I tried not to break down in front of them, I wanted them to be encouraged and I didn't want them to worry. I was blessed that I had just got my check that day, so I called a cab and sobbed uncontrollably when asked where are you going by the cab attendant. The holy spirit said go to the hotel down the street and pay for 2 weeks. I paid for 2 weeks and tried to make it as comfortable for my two boys as possible.

We had a microwave to prepare food but soon food ran out and we struggled to survive.

While in the hotel, we continued going to church and be obedient to God. We had ministries we were faithful in attending and we were trying to be hopeful.

After the 2 weeks was up, I cried out to the Lord telling him I couldn't do another two weeks here because we were hungry, I didn't have enough money to do this again I cried. The lord told me to pay for a week, by the fourth day I received a phone call from Angel, she was a girl I met at the shelter and we became friends. Angel was called the dirty girl, the stinky girl at the shelter because she and her kids never took showers.

They would have a foul mess in their room and no one would befriend her and often talked about her. I was different, I understood what It was like to be talked about and treated badly so I tried to help her. I would tell her we going to walk to the McDonalds and eat good, so let's get the kids looking nice.

Soon after she confided in me and told me she suffers from depression and found it hard to bath or comb her hair. So, I helped her. Often, I would keep her baby in my room and clean her. I got in trouble countless times doing that. The shelter didn't allow residents in each other rooms, so we would sneak. I loved her because I saw beyond her looks, I saw her pain. Angel had got her section 8 and had a beautiful house and was all moved before I had left the shelter so I was surprised to hear from her.

Where are you Angel said? I'm the hotel and begin to tell her what happened. She interrupted me and said I know, my mom wants to talk to you. I was confused as to what her mother wanted because I didn't know her mom. The lady got on the phone and said I heard about your story, getting kicked out the shelter for talking about Jesus. That's a shame, she said my daughter got a house can she call you? YES, I said excitingly.

Within 20 mins a lady called and told me she has this three-bedroom house and begin to tell me how beautiful it was, I really didn't care about the features I just needed a house. She kept talking about the yard, and the enclosed porch and all these things. Then she said I moved out and you can sublease.

Wow, ok I said how much money? How much to move in? She said the key is under the steps, just go there. I didn't think she heard me, I asked again how much I need, how much money? She said, NO MONEY JUST GO!! I instantly thought about what Kim said you don't need no money for a house just faith. I told the lady I would go and I cried out to the Lord a repentance cry for doubting him and having little faith. I thought about what if I wasn't nice to angel, I never knew she had my future blessing. Of course, I went on to pay rent at the house but it was very reasonable, no security deposit and I got a key to a house with NO MONEY.

I learned to never doubt God, even in adversity and being homeless he had a plan. From the church, I joined and was a member of for 7 years, to how God used me to minister to the shelter residence even while I was in the same position. How God taught me to love Angel when others considered her unlovable. It's amazing how other people testimonials blessed me even when I couldn't see the manifestation like they saw it. But, it reminds me of the power of testimonies and God's hand on our lives.

A few years later, I received a knock on the door at my home. It was my son's father. He begins to tell me how he was living in his car for the last few days and he needed a place to stay. I asked the Lord in my spirit and instantly he said no, just pray for him. I advised him I couldn't let him stay, and I thought about the phone call while I was at the shelter and he laughed at me at my lowest point in my life. Then I smiled in my spirit and was thankful I wasn't like him, and I had matured in Christ.

So, finally after he said a few choice words to me. He drove off with blasted music at full speed. Instantly, the holy spirit said pray for him.

So, I begin to text him a prayer, within 5 minutes he called me with a crying tone and said thank you. I knew at that moment I could never hurt him as he hurt me, I couldn't disappoint God.

Besides, whom else could give me miracles after miracle, favor after favor and love me unconditionally.

The Lord (the father) said to my Lord (the son, Messiah), "SIT AT MY RIGHT HAND, UNTIL I MAKE YOUR ENEMIES A FOOTSTOOL FOR YOUR FEET,"

Matthew 22:44

Six

I was 31 years old and I had been single a few years after living with my son's father for six years. The relationship ended peaceful, we simply out grew each other. So, my cousin and I was at the airport picking up my mom who just got in from Africa which she traveled frequently. So, as we laughed and talked as we made our way to the terminal to find my mother, two guys walked passed us and one guy said hey big booty. I turned around and immediately begin to check him about the nature in which he was coming at me, when my cousin urged me to give him a chance.

Reluctantly, I took his number and within a few days we begin to chat. He worked at the airport and within a few weeks of talking on the phone he shared he lost his job. This should have been an appropriate time to exit, but I didn't. I was intrigued by his ghetto demeanor and he's gangster style.

I was an upscale suburban woman with proper grammar and an amazing job. DeCarlo, would come over and we would smoke weed and ride around selling it. I thought he was the coolest, he would blast his music and pull up on his friends and was very popular. I had been a very structured type of women, I have never dated a thug before.

Soon, DeCarlo's would come over and stay nights at a time he soon moved in, weeks later I became pregnant but we were excited to be a family. He was very controlling and it was attractive. He cared about who I talked too so my phone calls were all on speaker. This was cute, I never had a man so attentive. He loves me, I convinced myself.

By this time, I was making six figures a year, and he was the neighborhood weed man. He never shared his money and I never saw an abundance of it, but he gave me the attention I so craved.

Within 5 months, we moved to a newer upscale apartment in a high-rise building. Now very pregnant and by this time, DeCarlo's is more and more controlling. He begins to insist on driving me to work, this only lasted for a brief time. He became enraged at the smallest things and called my job often to check and see if I was at work. It was almost like the more he showed signs of cheating the more abusive he got, both mentally and physically. Each day I would get smacked or hit, or some force of physical abuse. Then he would apologize, most often cry and try to buy me things.

At this point, right before my very eyes, he changed my self-worth, my confidence, my world. I wasn't allowed to wear makeup, he said you look like a clown when you do. He only wanted me in white t-shirts and gym shoes, he told me that made me look sexy. I begin to do anything he wanted just to please him, he was my best friend so I thought. He would go to the hair salon, and nail salon with me. Friends begin to question it and I would always dismiss them and tell them they are jealous; my man loves me that's why he goes everywhere with me.

He begins even going to the bathroom with me, because he said I was on the phone when I went in there so he wanted to make sure I wasn't talking to other men. He had no reason to think I was cheating, I've always been a loyal type of women. I tolerated his behavior because I thought if I can only reassure him, he's going to stop. If only I keep doing what he asks. Maybe one day he will stop fighting me and arguing with me. Maybe, just maybe he will stop.

DeCarlo's made me feel like I had no life without him. He would say, nobody wants you but me with all those kids. One day he will see I love him, I convinced myself. He loves me, but he just doesn't know how to show it, he comes from a lot of affliction I would remind myself. I would make excuses after excuses after excuses. The bigger I got in my pregnancy the more violent he became, soon I began to fear him.

On more than one occasion I would run away from him, I remember one day I ran down the hall as he chased me full speed.

I was screaming and knocking on everyone's door as I ran down the hallway. One lady finally opened the door one time and grabbed me and told me to be quiet as she locked her door to hide me. She must have been my angel, I've never been so afraid, he's going to kill me I said. The police were called and within a week, I would always let him back. He was all I knew, my family wasn't aware because he kept me isolated, I kept his rage a secret.

Soon I begin to find numbers in his phone and the women would describe my car as the car they met him in. His cheating had gotten so bad, one day it was four of us on the phone and everybody was saying he lives with them. One lady was a flight attendant so she was never home but proclaimed he was her man and lived with her. The other women worked midnights and said the same thing so because we all had different schedules, he could hide it very well. All these women were successful but none had stories of abuse only a little craziness from time to time, extreme jealousy but never abuse.

Why me? I thought. I comforted him about these ladies and like always he tried to argue and fight me, after a brief separation of only a few days again he was back. This time I begin to not give my car to him, so we argued about the car. One day we were driving down the street and by this time my license plates were in the window because he had snatched it off so much it was no longer able to be secured by screws.

So, in the back window it was displayed. This day we argued it was always petty arguments I have no idea what we were even arguing about. So, he snatched the plate out the window and refused to display it.

Well this was it, I was so tired of this man treating me badly, I was about 7 months pregnant and I have had enough. We were only a few minutes from my brother house and my brother had already told him to never hit me again. So, I thought it was time for him to have a man to man with my brother.

We pulled up and he begged me to not go get my brother. Apparently, he had heard my brother doesn't play games so he had the fear all over his face. To no Advil he must see my brother today because this got to stop I thought. I went in my brother Mike house and by the time I was telling him only a few things he was out the door comforting this man who have been fighting his sister.

Long story short no fighting, no arguing was done, only my brother telling him didn't I tell you not to hit my sister? All I remember was falling to my knees and screaming please don't kill him as the holy spirit instructed me to do.

I thank God that I was obedient because that day was going to be DeCarlo's last. My prayer was answered and he cried all the way home, proclaiming he was going to call his boys and get a gun etc. by the time we got home, I asked him if someone hit your only sister what would you have done? He looked at me and said you are right, I would want to kill him. I reminded him, I only have one brother with my mother and you only have one sister.

After that day, I had never ever, ever feared him again. The daily physical abuse stopped but not the verbal. So, I became physically abusive to him, the roles had reversed. I begin to say mean things and even fight him. This dysfunctional relationship lasted for another year until I finally left after continuing to see giving my all to him was useless. He didn't know what love was so he certainly couldn't love me the way God intended for a man to love a woman.

I learned when we allow a man or woman to abuse us, it's so much deeper than the abuse. My lack of selflove was the issue. The accepting of abuse was just the outward manifestation of me trying to receive love, even if it hurts. That's why subconsciously women will stay in this type of abusive relationship year after year and will try to convince themselves that this is normal, or just a phase. But, the most powerful thing we can reconcile in our brain is, he loves me.

That potential love will keep us in bondage, and the only way to loosen us is a spiritual awaken of Christ, and his love towards us. When we think of the love God has for us, it allows us to look at ourselves differently. In my relationship, I wasn't at my full awakening period, but what broke that chain off me being complacent with this dysfunctional relationship was him constantly doing more and more hurtful things without fear of the consequences of losing me as a partner.

The more I watched as he lied, cheated and lied and cheated I decided to give him more of what he wanted, I thought this would cure the need to seek other people. Once I bought a white woman home from work. She had never been with a black man and was intrigued by the idea of me introducing her to such a thing. So, one day after work we surprised him and I told him he could be intimate with her because I loved him and I wanted to please him.

Although I had no desire to sleep with her, or join I carefully watched to see if he would really go through with it. They begin to be intimate and very sexual right before my very eyes, I sat there feeling lost. He invited me to join several times and I declined. I was almost sickened by the fact I approved such foolery, I was faithful to this man for over 5 years and he could easily sex someone right before my eyes. After the quick five-minute session, I knew it was over with us but this familiar spirit embalmed my soul.

I didn't want to experience this type of pain with the next guy, I should just try to make this work. Within 3 days I discovered he's been calling her. I confronted her one day on her break as she was laughing on the phone, as I grabbed the phone I heard his voice. This was the last straw, I gave you the best of me and even someone else and you still feel the need to creep. I was furious and angry, it leads to her making a complaint about me because she was fearful of me I guess.

I couldn't understand why, my aggression was more towards him but I'm sure thinking back on it, I didn't make the work relationship pleasant.

She told the supervisor the entire story which was too much information to be told at a work place. Within a few weeks, I kicked him out the house and that was the spring of 2007. I never looked back again, as I ponder now on why did I stay so long. Why did I do so much to keep him, all I can say is I truly lacked the ability to see myself as God saw me.

To all those people whom are in awe of my transparency. I would say to you, had someone came to me and was transparent, I don't think half of my mistakes would have happened. Now since they did, if I can bless one soul to think before they get in deep into a dysfunctional relationship I have done my job. Only God can judge me!

I only wanted to tell half my testimony on YouTube and I remember after making the first video, that I couldn't go half way with God. If I was going to minister to his people I had to go all the way and tell it all.

Don't worry you can remain a private person but there will be a time in your life, you will be forced to tell your testimony of the darkest things in your life, you will be arrested in the spirit. To me this means you are no longer in control of yourself, Gods will be done within you and your spirit is arrested in obedience.

Ladies, if you have suffered domestic violence this testimony was for you. As tears stream down my face I want you to know you're not stupid, or slow. You have nothing missing or lacking, victory is all within you. You must overcome and greatness, that is your portion. You will be victorious, remember somebody didn't make it. To you the young lady whom is in that relationship and he's too controlling, watch the signs.

I pray this testimony blesses you with transformation via the Holy Spirit in Jesus Christ name.

I declare the devil is a liar, we will TELL the people how God got us over.

How God has saved and kept you and how God is blessing you right now to accept your past and embrace your future. People will talk about you, so what they talked about Jesus Christ. They don't have a hell or heaven to put you in, today I'm your voice and I declare NO MORE SECRETS.

Come to me, all of you who are tired from carrying heavy loads, and I will give you rest. Take my yoke and put it on you, and learn from me, because I am gentle and humble in spirit; and you will find rest. For the yoke, I will give you is easy, and the load I will put on you is light,

Matthew 11:28-30(GNTD)

SEVEN

Other secrets we hide are from undercover brothers. I've dated men and the past and I know for a fact today they are gay. I'm still friends with a few and I've never told them I know their secret.

They are attractive, successful and you would never know it by looking at them with the naked eye. You must know how to discern people with your spiritual eye. There are so many men that are undercover brothers, and there is reason why they have two life styles. Some are in secret because they haven't told nobody that their uncle touched them or that their dad or step dad raped them. It's a spirit of shame that have come over them that have been tucked away so they won't have to deal with it.

COME ON OUT!! I declare and decree this book will release the power to defeat Satan assignment over our secrets and we will see that God is in everything, he has power and dominion over all things so we should not and will not be afraid to tell our testimonies and to SPEAK OUT!! The blood of the lamb washes us clean and we have nothing to be ashamed about.

In the African American community, this is such a taboo subject and the best kept secret. No more will we stay in bondage of our pain, today we receive healing. It's not your fight, in this book it's healing of knowing you're not alone. Please, don't ignore that it happened, talk about it and heal from the pain.

For we wrestle not against flesh and blood but against principalities, against powers, against the rulers of the darkness of the world, against spiritual wickedness in high place

EPH 6:12 (KJV)

EIGHT

I had moments in my life where I really needed the Lord, I had a relationship him but I knew nothing about his power within me.

One day I needed a word, I just dropped the kids off at school I had only a little gas and a few dollars. I was waiting on an important call and I needed to receive it today. I was discouraged, I was living at this shelter downtown Detroit and it was horrible.

I remember driving to Grand River and Southfield in Detroit, Michigan my home state. I said to God, I'm not moving. I'm not going left or right or leaving this light until you talk to me. The holy spirit said turn right and go into this fast food place and eat. I said eat? I'm not hungry, I'm in the shelter I barely have any money and you want me to go eat, I exclaimed. Again, he said go.

I reluctantly turned right and went into the restaurant I grumbled and complained as I waited to be helped. I kept saying in my spirit, go eat, I'm not even hungry.

The man came to take my order and grumpily I said can I have a number 2, I got my drink cup and begin to have a full-blown temper tantrum at the pop machine. I said go eat, I'm not even hungry this is stupid. I'm laughing out loud now as I remember how upset I was with God. I was still doing as he asked but boy was I grumpy about it.

Finally, I sat down and reminded him for the 20th time, I wasn't hungry. Eat, the holy spirit told me again. I remember taking a bite of my chicken strips and I can't even explain the taste. It tasted as though I was so hungry and this was my first meal of the day and it was needed to fuel me. Eating this was nothing carnal, it was like spiritual food meaning why did it taste so amazing beyond great food it was simply explicatable.

I didn't remember eating, it went so fast it was the best meal I ever had in my life. Before I could swallow my last bite, my phone rang. It was the call I've been waiting for, I remember getting in the car and I sobbed uncontrollably I said God I will never doubt you again, I will never complain again.

What I now understand that God's ways aren't our ways and his will isn't our will all the time. I wanted an instant fix and he wanted me to rest in him first. I was so grateful that even through me complaining he blessed me. He knew I would complain but I had enough faith in him to call on him, go where he had me to go and do what he wanted me to do even without understanding, the why.

That day I stop complaining as much, lol. I still have my moments but truly I have learned to obey the voice of God. He so amazing, I can't begin to tell you how our relationship grew stronger after that moment. Don't question God just be obedient to what he has you to do, besides he knows what's best for you.

In my distress, I called to the Lord; I cried to my God for help, from his temple he heard my voice. My cry came before him, into his ears.

Psalms 18:6

NINE

At my kid's school there were signs, don't enter wrong way. Well everybody thought they was stupid and nobody really obeyed the signs. So much so going into the school, I joined maybe 15 cars and we entered the wrong way. Upon leaving the sign says right turn only, again this is stupid I thought. Well Lord I don't see no police around, I'm going to go left.

Instantly the holy spirit said turn right. I said why God? Don't you see all those people turning left, why are you bothering me about this stupid sign. Turn right, again the Holy Spirit spoke now with a firmer tone and again I went to bargaining.

Lord, why do I have to turn right. Everybody else is turning left and you keep bothering me about this sign.

NORA, TURN RIGHT AND DO RIGHT said the spirit of the living God. In such a tone, I feared to keep bargaining with, I turned right so fast and cried. Lord I hear you. Ok, I'm going to turn right and do right.

What I understood about my walk with God, is I'm set apart. Even among ministers. I can't do what they do. I have ministry friends who's been ministers for 20 years and yet don't live holy. I have pastor and bishop friends who sin more than the congregation combined. I'm not judging them or saying I'm holier than thou but more than a few people have called me that. Why? Because they see I live according to God's word and I'm truly set apart.

Sometimes I wonder why he doesn't convict them as he does me. Maybe he does but I have a heart to please him, and a fear of disappointing him so holiness isn't an option for me, it's a lifestyle.

I remember watching just two minutes of the news speaking of the lead in the water and the flint crisis. The holy spirit telling me to go down to flint with a team and have a prayer walk. Not really having all the details as to exactly what the Lord wanted me to do. I begin to do what he asked and within an hour, I had collaborated with other ministries and groups and we set a date to go to flint.

The day of the event as we gathered in my home to load the U-Haul truck and pray. Everyone was praying in tongues and I only had the gift one time a year ago as I prayed in tongues for the homeless while at home. During this time of the prayer walk I had been in prayer for a year to have the gift resurface but during the time of the prayer walk no one knew about my prayers as they prayed in tongues I prayed without a thought of that gift.

Long story short when we arrived at the venue, a few seasoned ministers and bishops wanted to change the venue location because of the snow and they had spoken to a few residents in the area and got tips on the best area to serve. Before arriving to the venue, I saw a strip mall two mins from my original venue and the spirit of the Lord said here is where I want it to be. The leaders had come against me even feeling as though me being a new minister of only a few years should follow what they recommended. But do you know when God tells you something even if it makes no since to folks, even if you stand alone you never second guess what he said, only follow him.

With the most humbled posture I urge them to follow the vision the Lord has set forth and we prayed at that location following the holy spirit and when I tell you God moved.

We set it up like a car wash, people pulled up, got water and we laid hands on them all from their car but some got out their cars as well. The move of God we all saw in that short length of time as we served. We sang hymns and danced while awaiting cars. The donations we were passing out filled a medium size U-Haul full of water cases of water. God moved!! So afterwards, we were scheduled to go to eat but I could see some people declined our planned dinner their spirits seemed still upset about me not compromising what god told me to do. The next day, God revealed leaders within that circle was talking about me even challenging the God in me.

Within two days, of me crying out to the Lord hurt because I felt deceived. These were my sisters and brothers and if I'm doing something wrong, tell me and pray for me don't talk about me. I was hurt to the core and the Lord told me to let him fight the battle. It was hard, but I did. When I tell you one of the people who was talking about me called and said, you are a woman of God, I declare that every evil word that was spoken over you be return void. Wait, the same leader who was speaking evil, God not only used her to speak life to me but over me, JESUS!!

I couldn't believe it then the second person repented to me, and in front of others, such a humbling, courageous thing she did. The third person I bought their food, bought the shirt we wore to flint and they spoke badly of me too and God told me just close the door on them. The last person was a bishop he never got upset, he wasn't angry about my vision he simply followed in the most humbled way I ever saw a leader.

I cried that week, I passed my test. That Sunday I went to church and my cousin asked for special prayer, pastor prayed over her and the holy spirit told me to lay hands on her. With my pastor's permission I did, on my way home after church my spirit was still vexed for her. I began to pray again telling the devil you can't have my family.

That morning around 4 am, I woke up laying hands on my cousin I was battling so much in the spirit my mouth begins to speak in heavenly tongues, this lasted 3 days straight I could barely speak English.

God restored my tongues only after I learned how to love the unlovable. I had to learn how to love the people who talked about me and I couldn't say anything. I had to learn how to stick to God's plan although people was against me. He also gave me the best relationship with one of the leaders, everybody makes mistakes but it takes a true woman of

God to be humbled enough to repent. I rather have a lot of friends like her then any other friend, she's my sister. I also had to past test after test of love, then he gave me back the greatest gift. The ability to speak our heavenly language.

That week took my ministry and my life to a new level with Christ, not only did he give me the gift of speaking in tongues, I also can interpret tongues as one of my spiritual gifts I prayed for that as well. I learned when people talk about you, pray for them, because if you battle them then your being God and his not the author of confusion. If you want him to be your God let him, step out the way he truly will fight your battles.

This testimony was a very hard season in my life, I felt like everyone was against me and most people like to be liked. There are people right now that won't do ministry with me because they are jealous of the God in me.

It's very sad that I had to keep being lower and lower to people just so they can feel complete. Until God showed me to never be lower than anyone, just always take a posture of humility. But, it's ok to be bold and confident people will say that's not being humbled but most people aren't confident so you may intimate them.

Be the best you, and don't be apologetic for it. God created us all with a purpose, walk into yours even if your standing alone. Don't aim to please people, or change the vision God gave you because it doesn't make since to others, it doesn't make since to them because God didn't give them your vision.

Be bold in Christ and stand on his word and love the unlovable. Once you learn the art of love, God will fight many of battles for you and unleash your gifts of war and of the spirit.

The Lord will fight for you; you need only to be still

Exodus 14:14

But he manifestation of the spirit is given to each one for the profit of all. For to one is given the word of wisdom through the Spirit, to another, the word of knowledge through the same Spirit.

to another faith by the same Spirit, to another gift of healings by the same Spirit

to another one working of miracles, to another prophecy, to another discerning of spirits

To another different kinds of tongues, to another the interpretation of tongues

but one and the same Spirits work all these, distributing to each one individually, as He wills.

I Corinthians 12:7-11

TENTH

As a young adult, I developed a habit of smoking marijuana, by the time I was in my mid to late 20's up until my 30's I was dependent upon it. I was a cigarettes smoker so now that I had overcame that habit marijuana was my daily ritual. I would smoke a blunt a day and I would use my last to get it if needed. Growing up my mother and dad was a smoker so It was common in my family, but taboo in the Christian community. I hid my habit well, I use to even go to church and have the blunt rolled and ready for me when I got to the car. I knew I was wrong but the more I went to church the less I had time to smoke. I wanted to be involved with church activities and I was uncomfortable being high during those times.

I was a single parent and weed was my husband.

It was so bad my supplier was a manager over my apartment complex so I didn't have to go anywhere to get it, it came to my front door. He knew I loved the Lord and although I was getting high, I was always talking about Jesus.

I was awoken one night at 5 am in the morning, to his holy spirit. He said you are an Evangelist, and I'm taking 3 bad habits away from you. I knew I had a calling to ministry but I ran, but this had never happened where he told me directly what I was and what I wasn't going to do.

I instantly accepted the calling and he was right, the taste of the marijuana was gone so I flushed the remaining marijuana in the toilet and answered my call to ministry. Soon Dee begin to knock on my door, asking what's up you haven't called me all week, do you have another supplier? I replied no, the Lord took the taste out my mouth. I don't smoke.

He laughed and say stop playing you got another supplier, don't you? You were my best customer, Nora it's no way you can stop smoking cold turkey like that again I reintegrated that it was only by the grace of God. He walked away in disbelief.

A months later Dee wanted me to take him to get his tax check and offered me $50 to take him. I agreed and as soon as we got into the car Dee began to ask questions. He said Nora, you really did stop smoking huh? Look at you, your eyes not red or nothing.

I reminded him of what God told me and why I no longer craved weed. He said I don't really believe all that stuff people talk about. If God is real why is kids dying? If God is real why are people poor and suffering? I simply asked him, well who woke you up this morning, and who allows the sun to shine? He paused and sighed and got out the car to get his check. He got back in the car and he begin to say Nora yes, I believe what you said, I believe there is a God. So, I told him if he believed in his heart and confess with his mouth and believe in his heart that Jesus was crucified, dead and buried but on the third day he arose with all power in his hand. Do you believe that? He said yes excitedly and I told him by his confession of faith he is now saved. He was very happy and so was I.

My saying yes to the Lord had nothing to do with me, but so much to do with the others that may be blessed by yes. Dee could see what a transformation in Christ looks like. From a hypocrite to a servant of God.

God maybe calling you too, believe me I ran. I told him, I don't look like those people or act like them church folks. Little did I know I still don't look or act like them. I never was created to, I was only created to be the best me, through Jesus Christ our Lord and savior.

Your yes is bigger than you, don't forget the thousands of people who are waiting to read your book, hear your song or go see your movie. One day at a time, one act of obedience will change your life.

And without faith it is impossible to please God, because anyone who comes to him must believe that he exists and that he rewards those who earnestly seek him.

Hebrews 11:6

ELEVEN

You saw the YouTube video, your reading the book and by now you see how much affliction and pain I encountered with dating, relationships even marrying a bigamist. By this season on my life at 40 plus, now you guys don't need to know my age. (smile). Well you already know I have had enough bad decisions and I wasn't dating at this point and I wasn't interested. I was a new Evangelist, I was celibate and I was at a good space in my life. I had a prayer line and my life had completely turned around for the good. I was attending church and bible study and I was very happy.

One evening at bible study I testified like I always do but this time, I was more open and transparent. I shared that this was the first time I didn't have a man, but I was very happy full of joy. It was me and Jesus for the first time and it was amazing. I felt proud of myself and I was on cloud nine. Well afterwards our first lady approached me and said Nora, I'm proud of you for your new walk, that's very nice but you must have balance. If your husband was around you right now you would miss him because your closed off concerning meeting people. I disagreed and told her, no I'm good lady Jaime. Just me and Jesus I don't want a man. Again, she reintegrated and I agreed to be open. Besides she was someone I admired, her and pastor has been married a while and so I took her advice. I tried to date.

The first date I went on I knew he wasn't the one 5 seconds after sitting down so I was ready to go. Besides, being in Christ I now knew my worth so I wasn't going to waste my time anymore. I tried to date again and I knew he wasn't the one instantly, so I went back to not dating and it was just me and King Jesus again but I had so much contentment I was happy.

After a few months, later I was strolling my social media page and I saw this guy's picture, it was nothing I even felt before. It wasn't that he was attractive, I have had my share of attractive guys that wasn't it. It was something I couldn't explain about his pictures.

I begin to look on his Facebook timeline and It was a woman in a picture with him, I instantly felt like maybe this was his girlfriend and I went about my day. Maybe 6 months afterwards I had posted on my Facebook page how the bar food is the best food, but I wasn't going in there or something to that matter. He responded, it was the guy from the picture. He was flirting and telling me that he would go get the food for me. I instantly became angry, I felt like this jerk got a woman and he's flirting, I instantly in boxed him to comfort him. Hey why are, you all on my page and you got a girl. Shockingly he said what, I'm single.

I begin to tell him about the picture and he laughed and said that was my sister. In disbelieve I went to find the picture and sure enough it read it was his sister. I felt like an idiot but I was very intrigued to get to know Paul. We exchanged numbers and when he called he said wait before we start talking, let's pray. I was like Jesus, wow how nice is this. Before we would talk he would pray over us, before and after the call. Day 2, I was in the middle of purchasing a car, so everything was going wrong when Paul called I begin to explain that the bank is holding my money and this and that and he said wait, wait let's pray. Omg this was soothing to my spirit, this was nothing I ever experienced.

It was amazing talking to him, we were around the same age he was a firefighter of 17 years, excellent credit and had only one son who was a teen. He was all my hearts desires I have written down and put in proverbs 31. He was everything, I mean everything on the list. Wait, before I could get happy I knew in my past I've made so many mistakes so I knew I had to seek God for more revelation and the spirit of the Lord confirmed, Paul was the one.

I was so happy and surprised that finally I have met the man who is for me, the spirit of the Lord had never ever told me this concerning a man I was grateful. I was excited to get to know him but in my mind, I could release my walls and relax with him. Although we haven't met I prayed I was attracted to him in person.

I was hosting a speed dating event and invited Paul, and he agreed to meet me at the event. Only a few people knew we had never met, but everyone heard of him. After the event, just at the right time, I was loading things in my car and there he was, there was Paul. It was like a movie, I will never forget I tried to get to him and it seemed like forever it took to get to him. I literally jumped in his arms, and that begin a period of being inseparable.

We begin to date, spend the night over each other house. Although, I was a minister and I knew I shouldn't do overnights with Paul I was reassured knowing God said he was the one, it was almost like permission to love him at full capacity.

The relationship grew so fast, I always moved fast when dating but this time was different I thought. We had excellent chemistry and an awesome friendship. It seemed like I was dating my best friend. I soon begin to extend myself a lot to him. If he was hungry, I would rush to take him food. I remember when he had an accident and a board fell on him, while in the fire. He expressed he was ok, he just got burned little on his chin. I felt the need to see him, to make sure. He was so dear to me, and I couldn't imagine him suffering without me there to help comfort him. I went over there spend my last $20 on food for him, because he was my honey, and in my mind, I was his wife to be. When I arrived at was surprised at the way he let me take care of him, it made me feel wanted. I rubbed the cream on his chin as I reassured him, this was just one of many of days I would care for him. I loved him.

Soon Paul and I was exclusive as he would say, this meant we were not a couple yet but we were exclusively only seeing each other he exclaimed. This weird definition of our relationship didn't bother me, because I didn't need a title, he treated me as his one and only and we had no issues until my contentment being an exclusive mate ran out.

I started to notice that I gave more than him, not financially because he bought me things just as I bought him things, I'm speaking for more spiritual. When he is sick, I would be there and when I'm sick he would never come see about me nor text messages or anything. It begins to be a one-sided relationship. I would ask the Lord about it, and he would always give me a word. Most often he would tell me to be patient, or he would reassure me that Paul was the one and that I needed to stay in it. After a year of dating, I felt like I needed the title. I felt like Paul was a very honest man because it took him almost 10 months to tell me, he loved me so I knew he meant it. Whereas every other man would lie and just say the words just to reassure me.

I couldn't understand if God has spoken to this relationship future and if he was the one, why is it I wasn't feeling the love like I should be feeling, he wasn't going above and beyond to make me happy. Isn't this how a man in love should act, I became confused and very frustrated and cry out to the Lord and each time he would give me a word and often tell me more about Paul and why I should be patient. Eventually I begin to share with Paul the word the Lord gave me without even asking for permission first. So, I would tell him the holy spirit said you are the one.

One day at church as I sat in the choir stand the holy spirit told me to write this down, I begin to write you are a prophet. The holy spirit again reentered you are a prophet. This was very confusing because I was only an Evangelist for a brief time and I had no idea you can be called to operate in ministry as both an evangelist and a prophet. I will never forget this day it was Jan 31, 2016 it was my mother's birthday, so as I went home to get ready to go to her house to celebrate with friends. The spirit of the Lord told me, Paul isn't ready leave him alone. What? I was devastated and very confused and upset, I asked what do you mean he's not ready, you said he was the one. Over the period of 6 months the Lord would explain to me that we have free will and although I created you for him, he's not walking in holiness and he's not ready and then he said, I will create another out one out of dusk. I guess he gave me more of my future because I am a prophetess but I would cry and beg for him to fix Paul, make him right. I don't want anyone else because this is who you said was the one. I was confused but I still had clarity, clearly God has closed the door on Paul and me, but still I prayed for him.

5 years prior the spirit of the Lord had told me to move to Georgia, I declined and told him I never lived in another state I can't do that. Within 2-3 years later, I had just had a super bowl party and bought new big screens and furniture and the holy spirit says, move to Georgia. I said ok, I sold all my furniture and had a yard sale, I sold EVERYTHING even my pots and pans. Then I chickened out, and said Lord I can't move out of state, I don't know anyone there and my mom is here. I was almost there but not enough faith, then Last August of 2016 the spirit of the Lord spoke again go to Georgia, this was only weeks after he told me to let Paul go I will create another one out of dusk. I said yes and Amen and with $742 and our luggage in my trunk, me and my three-son's drove to Atlanta. This was difficult because I still loved Paul and I didn't want to leave my grown children and my new grandchildren who were

not born yet. For some reason I had peace, unspeakable peace and enough faith to obey.

I had a townhouse in Atlanta that I had a preapproval to lease, upon arriving there I was happy to see the townhouse in person but they had roaches. I was disappointed so I opted out of the lease after 3 days and I thought no problem we will find another home. God didn't bring me this far to leave me. a month later I was paying $1400 a month for a hotel with roaches, I was discouraged crying every day. It was $140 and up to even apply for most places so I was losing money at record speeds because I was trying to apply. I was trying to rush into a home to avoid the hotel cost not including food for 3 boys.

After about 2 months, I was depressed and stressed. I felt hopeless and miserable. Although people from my prayer line was sowing into me, I was still drowning financially. I had a prayer line for 3 years at the time and people who heard about me struggling would send western union and money grams to bless me. but, I often had to borrow and ask people I normally wouldn't ask, so the word got out on the streets to my family and friends and then they begin to talk about me. I fell off is what they would tell people, meaning I'm not doing well but in a more demeaning type of way. They would gossip and when the whispers got back to me, I would feel discouraged because these are the people that supposed to love me. I was at my lowest point in my life, I thought.

God sent me people I never met, primarily from social media who were pastors and bishops just to pray for me and me for them. This helped to lift my spirits because I had no one. One day I went to the front desk to pay and I asked how much was two days because I couldn't afford a week any longer. The clerk told me the amount and I think I was $7 short so I decided to only pay for one night and go to church. At church, we were having one of our first meetings, the church was new, the launch day hadn't even official begin. I was excited to be a part of a moving ministry.

When I arrived, it was a table with t-shirts for the ushers. I was an usher, I sat down and was moved by the holy spirit to go buy a shirt. That would have been most of my money, what about tomorrow? Something in my spirit had peace and I went and bought that shirt as though I didn't have a worry. After the meeting was over the pastor opened the floor for testimonies and questions. The holy spirit told me to testify, I avoided the word. Again, and again he kept telling me to testify. I raised my hand and begin to testify about how I came to Georgia with $742 and I'm in a hotel and I didn't have money but I have faith and I was happy to be a part of this ministry, and I started crying not out of sadness but out of hearing myself testify to the struggle.

Before I knew it, a lady got up and put a bill in my hand, I had no idea what kind of bill it was but the holy ghost took over my body and I begin to praise and dance. People begin to lay money at my table, they just start coming from everywhere I became so overwhelmed with the love, I begin to scream no, that's enough no. I now know that was $100 bill she sowed into me.

That night I left church with 2 shirts because I bought my son one too. I had $198 cash and a $5 Starbucks gift card. Later the spirit of the Lord reminded me that my monthly income is $1980, which was 10% of the seed I receive. He wanted me to know he was still on the throne, that he still had me. What if one person wasn't obedient, the number wouldn't have been $198 or a significant number to me. All those people were needed to show me how strategic God is when he moves.

Well within a few weeks I was again without money. One day I cried out to the Lord but this time was different. I didn't grumble or complain, I didn't beg for a house and pray for a blessing. I said Lord if this is where you have me to stay, for your glory I would do anything. If you want this hotel to be my address, father I will do it for you, because it's not about me, it's only about YOU! You know what? I meant it, I had gotten to the point nothing else mattered. God had me still ministering to the hotel maids, the homeless people in front of the store and at the nearby shelters. I would give them half my money. I give them food and took their contact numbers and try to find resources for them. Although I was practically homeless that didn't stop me from being a blessing.

After that intimate conversation with the Lord within a few days I got a call, from one of our leaders at the church that somebody had a house for rent. The price was too high for me, and in an area, I knew nothing about but I agreed to talk to the lady.

Mrs. Sam and I talked for 2 hours, not only did she say I'm going to give you the house, no application fee, no credit checks you've been through enough she said. She even lowered the rent for 6 months of my lease, and she lowered the move in cost. When I saw the pictures, she emailed to my phone, I ran around the hotel and cried, the house was everything I prayed for over the years. 3,000 square feet, 4 bedrooms 3 bath, 2 car garages, 2 living rooms, 2 levels, sunken dining room with fireplace, foyer room, vanity sinks, my bedroom has an attached sitting room in a gated community with a park and pool. I couldn't believe this was true, the testimony continues that I only had $600 plus dollars when I went to try to get the house, and the lady said no I already helped you out I need that amount I asked you for. I just checked out of the hotel, my car was full and the kids was in school.

The holy spirit told me to just go, so what am I to do now. Lord again I'm following you and this lady needs all this money. When I tell you within 3 hours people I never met was sending me western unions, God moved in such a capacity that night I got my keys.

What the enemy meant for bad God used for good, even God gives you something he doesn't change his mind but your actions can change your destiny. You can have a husband predestined for you and God will not force him or her to choose you. I learned that just because that person didn't choose me, that my destiny wasn't over, God said he will create another one out of dusk. That's just a testimony of his love, not just for me but for you, if you trust and obey in him. I learned don't never give a man wifey benefits unless you're his wife. We must never give a man our all unless we are in a covenant relationship with him.

There was another prophecy God spoke and again I released the word to the man without prayer. I'm learning to close my mouth and learn just because you're a prophet doesn't mean every word is meant to be released and I believe, the holy spirit will release a word to you and sometimes it's only a test to see if you can be quiet. Example, if I tell you this person is your husband will you want so much to tell that person that you don't ask me first, or can I use your heart's desire to get you to release a word. Remember God works in mysterious ways so we will never be able to understand why he does what he does, but we can just be obedient and pray before we release anything. I mean don't release anything without prayer.

God has showed me love in such a capacity I would never know without making my leap to relocate. He wanted to see if I would trust in him, even in affliction and to those whom think that wasn't God who allowed me to suffer let me enlighten you, God rules everything. Study the story of Job, he suffered and he did nothing wrong.

As humbled servants of Jesus Christ we will suffer but he will never leave us nor forsaken us and it's always for our good. In my affliction, I learned to trust him more, I learned to be grateful and I'm sure he wanted to see would I still share if I had nothing. I passed that test because I have a pure heart for people and I learned the art of love and giving. I find that in my struggle that's when God is closest to us, we just tend to ignore him and complain during it. God wants us to endure in gratefulness, humility and to always reference him as Lord and being ok with his will to be done even if it means living in a hotel, or in a one bedroom apartment. True wealth begins when you value your relationship with Christ over everything.

I had to value him over embarrassment, gossip, my feelings, my pain even over my children, over my wants, over my thoughts even over my own breath. When you can come to a

space in your life where you can give Jesus
Christ your ALL, then you have accomplished
defeating darkness and your purpose can be
revealed and fulfilled now that you're in the
light.

It's so amazing to get pass others
judgement of you and to leap when it doesn't
make sense to you or no one else. Your leap is
not about you, it's about the others that will be
blessed by you. My YouTube video was not
about me, my moving to Georgia was not about
me and this book, was less about me and more
about the transformation in Christ though me. If
you are not transformed by your testimony
then you will continue to go through more than
you have too.

My prayer is that you will see my
testimony as your avoidable suffering and you
can just be transformed by the renewing of your
mind, to realize Jesus is Lord and it's not about
you. It's for the next person waiting to be
blessed by you.

TWELVE

My oldest son had found himself in trouble with the law, that morning before court the holy spirit sent prophets and apostles to call me to give me a word from the Lord. I was full of faith leaving home, I knew God grace was upon us. Entering the court during a briefing with his attorney. She gave us shockingly disappointing news contrary to what we were told earlier. As I looked at his pregnant girlfriend and I thought of the idea of him missing the birth of his first child, I began to pace the floor.

I said Lord I need a word, Lord I need a word. The spirit of the Lord said Believe or Not, have Faith or Not. This blew my mind considering I was full of faith 10 minutes prior, the enemy is just that slick he creeps in just when you think your full of faith and he tries to devour your joy.

That day the judge said exactly what the apostle prophesized during my call with her. The judge said I don't know why I'm doing this, it's was even against the probation departments recommendation but I'm going to not give you any jail time.

Then he started saying everything I've been saying to my son as a parent. When are you going to marry her? You going back to school? All you heard was me, my son's girlfriend and her mom scream and cry out so loud. We just witnessed a miracle, the atmosphere felt anointed as the judged teased us for boohooing as he laughed. Even he knew the spirit of the Lord moved upon him. He was known as the strict no mercy type of judge but God is ruler over all.

I leave you with this Jesus loves you and he's is Lord!! So, let him be Lord over everything there is nothing too big for him.

Believe or Not, Have Faith or Not!

Made in the USA
Middletown, DE
29 May 2023

31084603R00060